To Judith,

On the occasion of your
Queen's Guide Award.

May 1983.

Ruth Nickerson

PROMISE OF DAWN

Pages from a Thailand diary

A LION BOOK

Copyright © 1982 Lion Publishing
Published by
Lion Publishing
Icknield Way, Tring, Herts, England
ISBN 0 85648 480 6
Albatross Books
PO Box 320, Sutherland, NSW 2232, Australia
ISBN 0 86760 364 X

First edition 1982

Acknowledgements
Illustrations by Ruth Nickerson
Photographs for 'One of the family' (final) and
'Tragedy' by Fritz Fankhauser. All other photographs
reproduced by kind permission of Tear Fund,
11 Station Road, Teddington, Middlesex, England,
and taken by Tricia Anderson, Jenny Loughlin, Tony Neeves
and Stephen Rand.

Printed and bound in Britain by Purnell and Sons
(Book Production) Ltd, Paulton, Bristol

Dedication

With special thanks to Nruas Hawj (Droua Her)
and Zeb Yaj (Jej Yang) who have helped me so much.

This book is dedicated
to all those at Sob Tuang Refugee Camp,
and all others throughout the world
who have 'no place'.

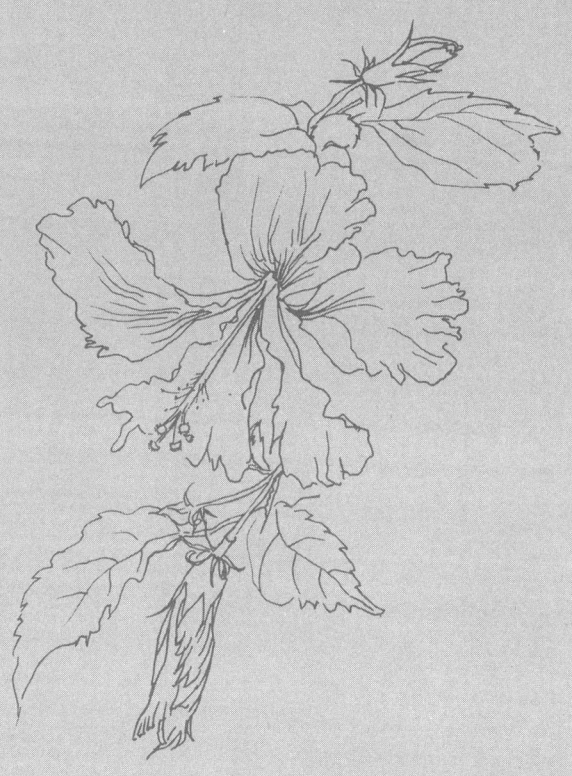

Contrast

A *milky-blue panorama of distant mountains and ridges forming the Thai-Laos border—the view is breathtaking. I'm astounded, almost shocked at the sheer beauty of the scenery of northern Thailand.*

I arrived in Bangkok three days ago. On this journey north, the flat central plains with their paddy-fields have gradually given way to more rugged terrain.

Somewhat apprehensively I travel up the valley to Sob Tuang for the first time. Clusters of thatch-topped houses form a patchwork pattern on the hillsides. Pictures in my mind seem to run riot as what I actually see vies with my preconceptions.

What a paradox! Does a refugee camp really exist in these picture-postcard surroundings? It seems a denial, a travesty of all expectations. But it is fact: This place of beauty is a refugee camp. Its location in no way lessens its problems—perhaps it even obscures its deepest human needs.

I turn to look again at the encircling hills and wonder if their intense beauty will lull me into forgetting the deep pain of these refugees. Or will it renew, refresh and help me, in some small way, to relieve their suffering? I pray that it will.

No easy answers

I had heard much about refugee camps. Before leaving England, the media had soaked every corner of my mind with the agony of crisis situations: emaciated, sick bodies, dying people, unbearable overcrowding, squalor and hunger.

But newspaper headlines change. After responding to the immediate crisis, public interest veers elsewhere. Long-term involvement is a very different and far more demanding matter. When the starving have food and the sick have medicine—what then? Some refugees have been at Sob Tuang for five years, unable to return home, unable to move on. Some have left to try to adjust to a new life in the USA, Canada or France. There are no panaceas, no easy answers.

The heartbeat of humanity

Sob Tuang... high up in the hills, browned and parched by the heat. The hot wind blows over the winding road and sweeps the earth into the undergrowth. Once-bright yellow flower petals lie coated in thick dust. Leaves are choked as they struggle for growth.

It is the hot season. Between the walls of the bamboo houses pigs sprawl and sleep in the sun-hot shadows. Dogs scavenge along the pathways... hens peck at fallen rice-grains. Children are playing in the dust as I walk past. Sometimes they stand and stare. The small boys

look with solemn questioning, then, before they run away, burst into laughter.

And everywhere there are people. People watching, talking, sharing secrets, sifting the silences. I marvel at the intricate cross-stitch embroidery on their clothes. Women with young babies carried in cloths on their backs mount the ridge. The footprint hollows made in the ground fill with dust almost immediately.

In the lazy heat I can catch snatches of conversations. I hear languages I don't understand. But through the sounds and scenes I start to feel the heartbeat of humanity. I begin to identify with its joys and poignancies. I begin to see its sicknesses, to hear its sighs. I'm here—here at Sob Tuang. I can feel both its hope and the pulse of its fear. Sob Tuang is becoming part of my life.

Sob Tuang …
Lending your paths to my wandering,
And sharing the throb of what you are
With all my questionings.
I pause, in the privilege of being with you,
Stranger that I am,
Trying to understand …

So much to learn

I've been at Sob Tuang almost two months. Today I was asked to help with allocating used clothing to the refugees.

The distribution took place in a large building known as the 'meeting hall'. It has a concrete floor, wood-slatted 'open' sides and a roof of corrugated iron. The secondhand clothes came from many sources, and were given to those whose needs were greatest. Warm sweaters and jackets are

Saturday
December 8th.

Think this is some kind of
Convolvulus, - Bindweed -
(or thai "Morning Glory"?!)

Grows by the road side
and is v. common locally.

desperately needed during the cold season when temperatures drop during the night and early morning, and mists hang low on the mountain-sides.

Many people came and the crowd stayed all morning. We distributed clothes to over 200 people and still the number of faces looking in from outside seemed no fewer.

I was tired and grew impatient. I lost interest. How I wished they would all go away. Sorting through the piles of clothes, trying to match garment to person, made me fractious. Irritation slowly grew into resentment. The care and concern I had felt at first melted away.

In shame I remembered the words of Jesus: 'When I was naked you did not clothe me. Anything you did not do for one of these you did not do for me.'

I knew I had failed to express God's love in action. Immediately I was deeply sorry, and I asked God's forgiveness. To say I am committed to helping those at Sob Tuang, and to be committed are, I now know, two very different things. I have so much to learn.

Christmas at Sob Tuang

The hills were hazy in the heat. As I walked from the school up the dusty bank to the hospital building, thoughts of Christmas edged their way into my mind.

I entered the ward and sat on the end of one of the beds. Watching all the people there I saw a Hmong refugee mother with her small child. Contentedly he sucked at her breast. She held him close and joyously rocked him. The time of year and the scene before me made me suddenly and acutely aware of the birth of Jesus.

There were no swaddling bands for this Hmong child. There was no manger bed. His mother wore no Mary's robes. She wore her tribal clothes—the bright red sash, the black jacket with sleeves of banded green. These spoke to her of home. I watched. She lifted up the child. He was so close to her. She smiled, and lovingly rested her lips on his cheek. He responded, curled his small fingers to her touch, turned and looked up at her. He felt her love and, knowing it, slept, securely cradled in her arms.

I looked out of the windows to the far hills which encircled the camp. Not Bethlehem's hills. Not the place of

shepherds' flocks. No herald angels praising God. These were the distant mountains of the Thai-Laos border. Closer at hand were the hills of Sob Tuang scattered with forest trees and sun-silvered pampas grasses. Here the sloping valley-sides sheltered many who had walked the trails to find a place, a home.

I paused in the midday heat. My thoughts were on Christmas, on all the way Mary and Joseph had walked. I remembered the birth of Christ so far away from home amongst strangers. Then, slowly, deliberately, I looked back at the Hmong mother and her son and paused—to thank my God for his Emmanuel.

Grasses at
Maejarin.
Thailand

Into this day, loving you Lord
Knowing that you love me,
I bring thanksgiving as I ask for grace
To serve you, and obey, remembering
You said: "Apart from me, you can do nothing."

Into this day quietly, with you Lord
As the light dispels night's shadows
And the dawn offers its gift ... the morning,
For your renewed mercies.

Into this day, gently, with you Lord,
Your strength made perfect in my weakness
Making it so
I watch the grasses bend to the breeze ...
So let my spirit yield to you,
Resisting not your touch

Into this day, following you Lord,
I am your disciple, learning ....

'Some place for my life'

The pain and poignancy of the refugees' situation can often best be captured in their own words—comments and questions from the heart which will stay with me for the rest of my life:

'How long would it take to walk to America?'

'It is dark, the future is very dark.'

'We have no things to use, we cannot go anywhere. We want to live in Thailand but we can't. There are so many problems every day—today, tomorrow and the next tomorrow. Today is over now but we don't know about tomorrow.'

'What shall I do? What is best for me to do? Will the people be kind? Do they like refugees?'

'Excuse me teacher Ruth, what is a space-ship?'

'There are many questions in my life. Why are there many poor people?'

'What else can I do? I cannot go back. I cannot stay here.
I am a refugee, I have no place. I must go. I must start a
new life, and for my sons.'

'My mother died. I am very sad.' (One of my Class 6
pupils, Wanna, wrote this at the bottom of a spelling test.)

'I'm leaving for California on Monday. Please come and
say goodbye.'

'I watched some of my family packing all our things, and
some of my shirts. We fetched big boxes from the market to
put clothes in, like that box there. I turned my eyes away,
I couldn't bear to look. I felt sick inside. I thought about
them going away, and I was sad. I will not see them.'

'My grandmother does not want to go to America. She is
ninety years old and says she cannot learn English.'

'If I could, I would like best of all to have
some place for my life.'

Children playing

Children playing. . .here at Sob Tuang, as they would
anywhere in the world. I watched them. The fact that this
was a refugee camp held little significance for them.

Those who had crossed the Thai-Laos border some
years ago had now perhaps forgotten much of the long and
hard journey through the forest. Drugged into quietness,
they had probably slept through much of it, lest they
should cry and betray the exodus. For many children this
was their home, their birthplace. The insecurity of the
camp spelt security to them.

Their games amused and intrigued me. Inventiveness
transformed discarded batteries and a sloping trail into a
race-track, where two boys repeatedly rolled the batteries
down and scrambled to retrieve them. A ripped plastic
water-container was the sled on which a child slid down
the dusty banks in obvious joy. Smaller children revelled
in the delights of puddles and thick mud. Young girls
tossed a stone into the air, then grasped as many short
sticks as possible before it fell again. Others spread white

ashes on the hard-packed earth for a game which closely resembled what we used to call 'hopscotch'.

Children playing…here at Sob Tuang, as they would anywhere in the world. Children do not think of future days. Life is for now, for play, for this essential moment. And as they grow up—what then?

'We can think about our children every day, and what will happen. We can think about them and every time we will be sad. It is better not to think. Everyone says "perhaps…perhaps". No one can tell us what will happen. It is better not to think.'

YOUNG GIRL FROM YEO TRIBE

The shock of death

I *had never seen death before.*

The first thing I heard was the wailing. The walls of the hospital were a barrier to sight, but not to sound. It was unmistakable. Death. There was the drone of grief— chanting followed by weeping. As the body was carried out, the wailing became louder. The bereaved family of the refugee followed. Death. It was all so different from what I had imagined. The impact of seeing a dead body for the first time startled me. Momentarily I felt stunned.

The 'hearse' was a Toyota pick-up. I watched the men move the spare tyre from the back to make room for the body. After they had lifted up the corpse then laid it down, some of the family climbed up and sat on either side of it. There was no room for the rest. They turned, and filed away 'home' along the trail, up, and across the hills. I watched them go, and felt their numbness. One of the men in the truck turned the blanket back to look at the face. Was it the same? Yes, the features were the same, but there was no life.

The truck revved noisily, moved off, turned the corner and was gone.

What pathos. They had fled from their homes hoping, one day, to begin a new life. Now death in the family had punctured that hope.

I believed God cared. Could I still believe it witnessing this suffering? A new silence filled my mind. I had seen death. I had learned more about life. I still believed God cared. God has not divorced himself from that suffering. He suffers too. The world is his, his creation and he identifies with it. It is far beyond my understanding, impossible to explain. But God does care. This conviction renewed my own response to be involved in helping to relieve suffering for his sake.

Jan 12 th

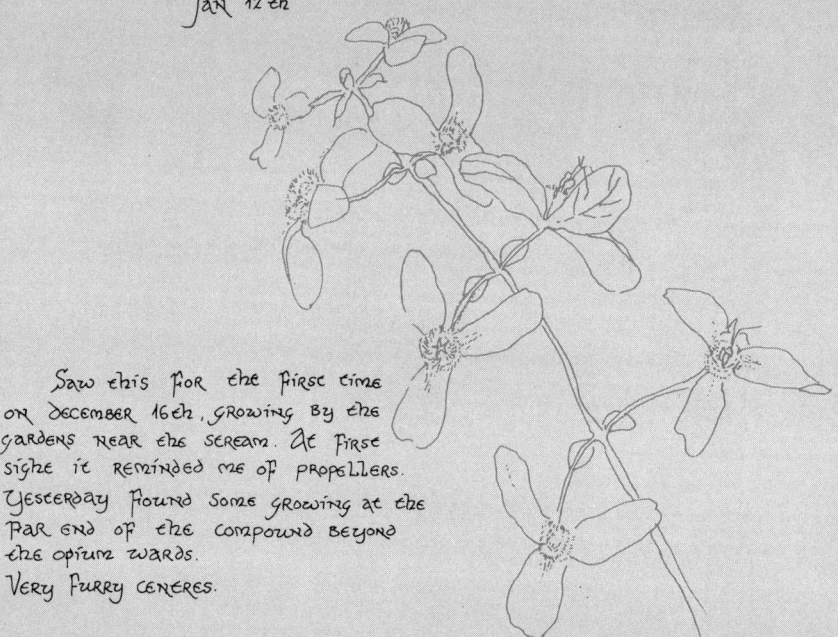

Saw this for the first time on December 16th, growing by the gardens near the stream. At first sight it reminded me of propellers. Yesterday found some growing at the far end of the compound beyond the opium wards.
Very furry centres.

To live again

It began one evening in early March. A tell-tale line of orange flame licked its pathway over the rounded shadows. I followed the gradual movement of the glimmering fire that marked the burning of the hills. In the hours that followed, the whole valley choked with thick smoke. Everything was charred and blackened, branches of trees like pyres, small heaps of white ash were scattered over desolate hillsides.

Days later the pungent stench of burning still filled the air. Heat, dust and smoke…and the smouldering ground scorched again by the sun.

As I went up to Sob Tuang and saw the devastation,

I could not imagine that the hills—a huge, blistered, still-hot scar—would ever be green again. The silvery-headed grasses by the roadside were no more than tattered remnants. Trailing tendrils of blue smoke still rose to the sun.

It seemed impossible that these hills could live again, so great was the extent of the fire.

When the first rain came it was a sudden storm in the night, a catharsis for the hovering sultry oppression of the day's heat. Intermittent thunderclaps split the night. The sound of rain beating its deluge onto long-hardened earth was deafening.

At dawn the hills knew a forgotten freshness. I smelt charred wet grasses drying in the warmth, saw sunlight water droplets glinting on battered leaves. In the stillness of morning there was the promise of restoration.

Only a short distance away from this renewal in nature were thousands of people living in the camp. Theirs was a different kind of desolation, and they too wanted new life, new beginnings. While the renewal of plant-life would quickly take its natural course, for people the process would be infinitely harder.

Just another day

I decided to ride the Yamaha up to camp even though I remembered from yesterday the slippery mud on the unsurfaced road. It stopped raining just before I left the house for another day's teaching. I rode cautiously. The road now so familiar, the sight of the beautiful morning clouds low down the valley-sides have never lost their attraction.

I arrived (thankfully without too many skids) and went to my first class, teaching to the usual accompaniment of banging and hammering and conversations, of younger classes chanting Thai in chorus. No problems explaining 'splash' and 'puddle': the cement floor of the classroom was flooded again. Other words were harder for students from a hill-tribe background: 'bathroom', 'tractor', 'train', 'piano'. I drew a keyboard on one of the desks with chalk and sat down to 'play' in an attempt to explain. The only music produced was the laughter which convulsed us all!

We stopped after morning school to eat rice, and today I spent the rest of the break practising reading Thai. Perhaps I have become much more used to lack of privacy now, though I still long to be alone and quiet at times. Solitude is rare and very precious. Afternoon classes brought home once more the value of understanding more of the students' language and way of life, especially trying to learn the names for family relationships, so important to them.

Sue Wue came as arranged after the last class to plan Neng Xiong's next lesson, make the visual aids and practise the dialogues. During that hour black clouds gathered, and as we finished it began to rain again. I had planned to go with Droua to visit an unexplored area of the camp, but we delayed our departure, and he told me some of the Hmong traditional folk stories about Zab the cunning servant who always outwitted the king. I was fascinated—and almost glad of the rain!

Once it had stopped, we began walking towards the ridge but paused by one of the official buildings to read the list of fifty families due to leave Sob Tuang (for resettlement in the USA) in four days' time. A Yao man standing by was deeply distressed. I realized that ten of his family were going, while he and one other would be left behind. How I ached inwardly for the pain which hurt him so much and for the grief so clearly seen in his eyes. My own recent partings from friends and family smarted in response. I could in some small measure understand and share his tears. On the ridge I looked across to the eastern range of hills spanned by a huge rainbow arc, the symbol of hope, and I thought again of the Yao refugee. Could he still hope in the bitterness of his experience?

As we left and walked along the path I was reminded of yesterday's fish ration being distributed. No fish were to be seen now, but despite the rains, a strong smell was evidence enough. We proceeded down the wet and muddy trails crossed by small streams and passed the wells which the refugees had made, finally reaching our destination—the house of the White Hmong dentist. I was disappointed not to find him at work, but he willingly talked about his methods for replacing broken or missing teeth, pausing occasionally to smoke his large bamboo water-pipe.

I returned to the fork in the path with Droua. He went home, and I walked back through the camp, collected the bike to return to the valley. The near-sunset sky on my right was a band of glowing light just above the far hills, contrasting with heavy, dark, blue-black cloud above. Teaching was over for the day, but the evening still lay ahead…end of term exams to set…perhaps some letters to read, or visitors at the house…

God understands

The reason I find myself at Sob Tuang is because I believe God wants me here. And when I feel my own resources are inadequate, I know that he understands and enables me to carry on despite the difficulties. But I cannot help wondering how faith in God works itself out in the lives of refugees who have become Christians.

Today after school I chatted with Sang Boon Ma, a Lao girl whose Christian faith is real and meaningful to her in her situation as a refugee in Sob Tuang Camp. She shared with me the difference that being a Christian makes to her:

'Because I am a Christian, when I am in Sob Tuang, when I am in Laos, wherever I live in the world I know God understands. When my heart is very troubled, when I am busy with many things to think about, many things I don't understand, it is all right, because God watches and sees, and I can explain to other refugees about Jesus.'

Siam Weed
grows in abundance where "slash + burn" method has been used to clear ground.

Her name is Yee

This child. I have seen her often. She walks towards me unsteadily through the shady pathways where dogs, asleep, lie motionless, where hens peck in the dips and crannies for rice grains, fallen from the winnowing trays. She does not carry her baby brother on her back—a pretend carrying-cloth contains a rolled-up piece of blanket.

This child. She wanders on the trail alone, stoops to feed leaves to a tethered pig, then as she stands, stumbles. No cry. She is clumsy in her movements, sudden with smiles. She is laughed at and left alone to play. Who cares?

This child, one of so many, with her dirty face and filthy clothes, looking at me with questioning eyes.

This child, forgotten twice over, this is Yee. And for Christ's sake I remember and I care.

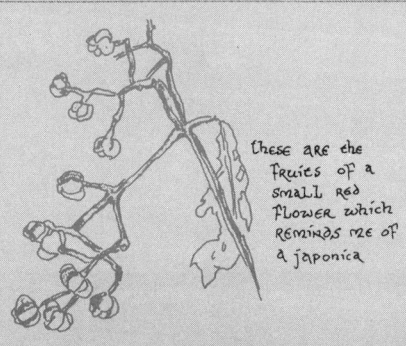

these are the fruits of a small red flower which reminds me of a japonica

Freedom-flight

It was midday. I wanted to find somewhere quiet where I could be alone—just for a while. The camp was always so full of noise, and people, and activity.

I walked to the far end of the market and found the place I was looking for up on one of the hills. From there I looked down into the valley. There were two huge birds circling far below. I watched fascinated. They wheeled and soared in curves that seemed to span the mountain-side. I was magnetized by their grandeur, and could not turn my eyes away.

Glorious freedom! They caught the wind's lift, swooped again and flew higher. They were free. Free to fly in sweeping arcs across the ranges. Free to fly over natural forests and man-made borders. My whole being sang, and I felt as if my own soul reached out to join them in their rapturous freedom-flight.

Two birds upborne in flight over the valley. A familiar sight. Perhaps an even more familiar sight to the refugees who had crossed the border and had come to live at the camp. But what did they feel as they watched? The birds were free to go to wherever they wanted—but people? No.

My thoughts spun and I found myself searching to understand freedom. Who is truly free? I knew then that true freedom is not confined by outward circumstances, but is only to be found in Jesus Christ.

ae hua bin at the 'Juniper tree'
Shrub in the garden
Flower petals a deep but delicate
pink with an inner "fringe". ragged
and veined with thin streaks of
darker pink.
Beautiful white feathery 'spiral'
in the centre

The cost of loving

So they have gone...
The dusty clouds hang on the morning air
Each particle suspended, but a moment,
Slowly to settle again.
The crowds disperse,
Back to the market-place.
Or, farewells said, return 'not comforted'
To empty sorrowing...
They are bereaved, and hilly beauty
Flecked by the morning sun is lost
For grieving eyes.

    The memory lingers on the final touch,
    The handclasp given,
    The arm full stretched to reach another's
    Fingertips,
    The features in the face
    Of one beloved,
    Then lives it through again, as if
    To grasp its clarity
    For all time.

There on the path she stood, aged and bent,
Apart from all the crowd,
To watch in silent grief the exodus.
Her face, drawn in the unwept tears
That craved for liberation.
Parting...
Parting from...
Parting from part of herself, in them;
The cost of loving—
Weakness was her strength,
She watched them go.
I saw her age-worn face, and read its pain.
No words were said.
The silence spoke, and was her cry.
And could I understand?
For her I wept within the moment's
Touch on time,
And silently we walked away.

A time to heal

The speed and abrupt stop of the clinic Land Rover signalled an emergency. The rear doors were opened, and the young man, lying on a stretcher, brought out. His left foot, ankle and leg were bound tightly with strips of cloth secured by a chain-link belt. One of the nurse-aides told me he had chopped through his foot while cutting wood in the forest. I swallowed hard at the thought of it.

Then, as I looked, I recognized this refugee. It was Yang Sao, a student from the fifth form, to whom I taught English daily. I watched apprehensively as a nurse untied the cloths. I saw the deep gash.

They took him to the operating-room. Should I go too, or stay and wait? Indecision was brief. I went in and was relieved to hear that he would not suffer permanent lameness.

In the ward, later, he told me how the accident had happened, and spoke of his intense fear. 'I thought I was going to die. I was afraid. I was very afraid.' We talked together briefly of the Christian assurance of life beyond death.

Six months later, Yang Sao left Sob Tuang to be repatriated in the USA. The departure scene at the camp had become familiar, but the poignancy of partings retained its sharpness. Crowds of relatives and friends surrounded the coaches. Many wept unashamedly.

The pain was real, very real. No sharp-bladed axe was visible, no apparent injury. This wound would take much longer to heal.

One of the family

I watched the everyday family life of those at Sob Tuang
with great respect and admiration. I looked at the women
as they breast-fed their babies and saw the beautiful
response of mother to child, of child to mother. Family life
extended beyond the parents and children to include
others in a close-knit bond. The elderly were valued and
honoured; the sick or disabled were not ostracized. They
had a real place in the family too.

At times I felt deeply disturbed as I thought about the
raw shock which many of these people would experience
when they left the camp for repatriation in a 'third
country' in the West. The contrast was so stark—between

Yao baby at the camp hospital.

their old way of life in Laos and now here in the camp, and what they would face in the future. Despite the amazing human capacity for readjustment, I found myself wondering if the gap would not prove too wide to bridge.

There was a beautiful simplicity about their lives. Life can be lived without so many of the things we have come to regard as essential. I thought of people in the wealthy, developed countries striving to discover a simpler, more satisfying life, stripped of trappings. And yet, there was no way that the refugees who left for a third country could be protected from all that creeping materialism had spoiled.

It was impossible at times not to make comparisons. I knew the pressures of commercialism in other societies, the strong but subtle persuasion to accumulate more and more material possessions, the unhappiness and dissatisfaction bred by this acquisitiveness. I was also keenly aware of the increased number of broken homes, the disintegration of family life—and the social problems those tragedies caused.

I ached inside as I thought of those who had already left Sob Tuang, and of those who would follow. How would they cope, suddenly confronted by fast-moving, twentieth-century, Western society? Would they face misunderstanding, fear, hostility, prejudice?

But what alternative was there? Life in a refugee camp offers no stability or security. But the distress of the refugee does not end when he leaves the camp. It goes on. I prayed that in their new environment there would be those who would understand, those who would help them to settle and adapt and begin to feel like one of the family again.

Refugee house made from bamboo/thatch/
woven leaves/bits of cardboard.
Had a marvellous time drawing this—
everyone gathered and it was a real
'community' interest for children and
adults who watched as the drawing
took shape and they recognised it.

A spirit of giving

Those who came to Sob Tuang were not allowed to possess any land of their own to farm, so rice and other staple foods were regularly distributed. They could not collect adequate supplies of firewood, so charcoal was provided. Medical treatment, basic equipment and education were all given free as part of the overseas aid programme.

Yet, in the midst of all this dependence on outside help, there remained a true spirit of real giving—giving out of deep poverty. It never ceased to amaze me, and to be my example.

Insoow, the elderly Hmong grandmother, regularly brought me gifts of cooked rice, meat, a piece of sugar-cane or a root vegetable. She gave gladly. Her loving generosity extended beyond these tangible gifts, and the welcome to her home. Insoow, will you ever know that out of your poverty you have enriched me so much? You shared your skills, your heritage and your own self.

Pattern for life

Lessons are over. The sun burns hot into the loose
earth as I walk to Sang's house. She is weaving at the loom
set below the stilt-house in the area of Yao refugees.

It is shady here and I sit beside her as she works.
We talk as I watch her moving the carved boat-shaped
shuttle across and between the white warp threads, and
I am fascinated by her skill. The pattern forms: diamond
shapes of emerald green criss-crossed with angles of white.
I admire her work. She pauses. Her smile is the token of
our friendship.

'In Laos we did not buy cloth, we always made it.
I learnt as a small child, watching my mother then
trying for myself.
You would learn too! You would remember!
But perhaps it is not important for a foreigner . . .'

Sang turns to concentrate again; I see her strong swift
hands . . . then glance at the sun-filtered leaves, green
diamonds against white clouds. The woven cloth would be
beautiful anywhere, but because it has been woven here,
its beauty is enhanced. Yes, surely it is important to create
something of beauty and of worth out of a situation of
tragedy. It is very important, and it is possible.

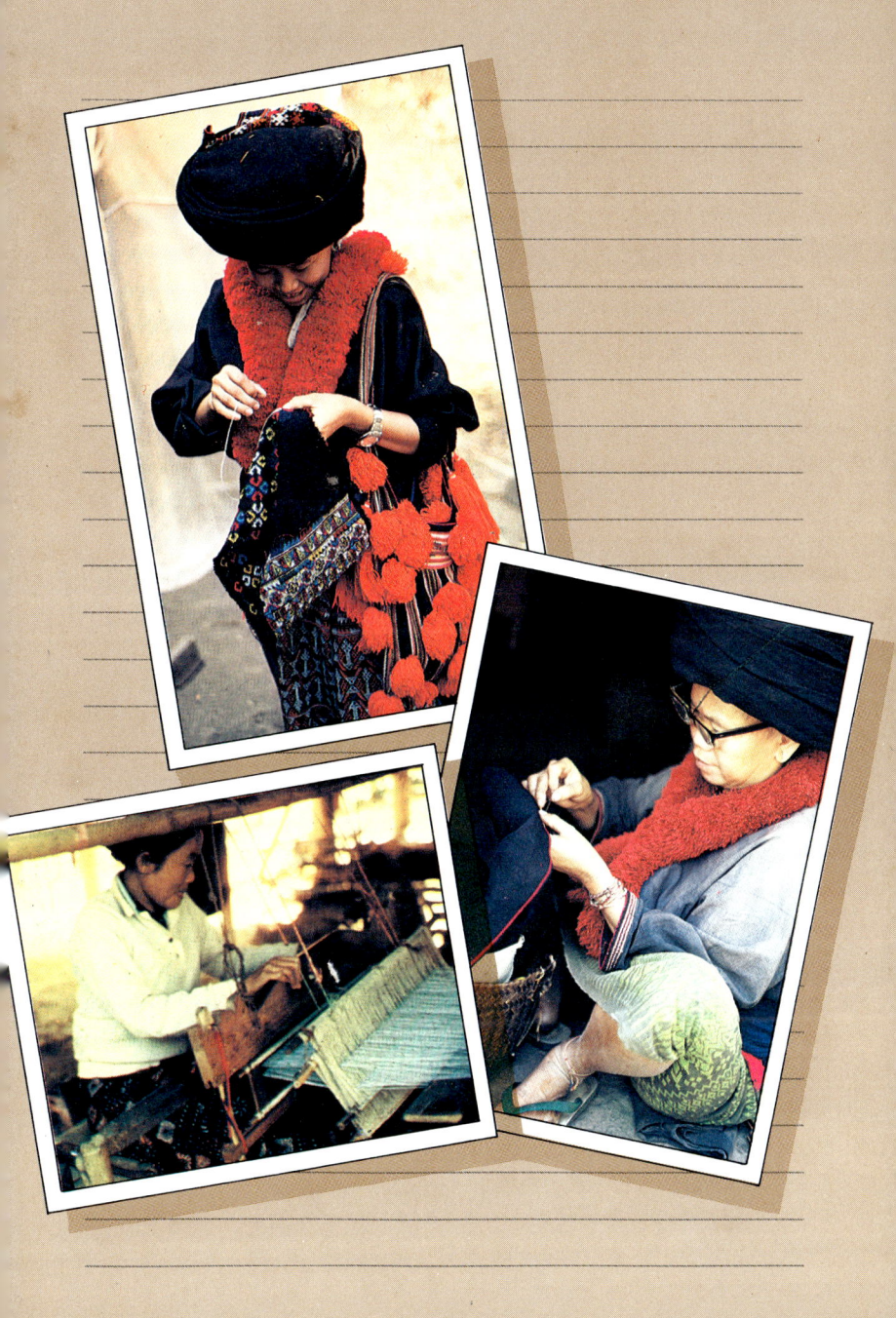

Tragedy

In early July continuous heavy rain fell for three days causing widespread flooding in the Maejarim valley and Nan plains. Lives were lost and thousands of bahts' worth of damage was done. At this time of year heavy rains were expected, but the torrential rain of these few days without a single pause was very different. The Nam Wa river overflowed its banks and grew to a turbulent, seething

torrent. Its rampaging flow swept along huge branches, logs and débris, eroding all in its path, destroying our pump-house and numerous bridges. I stood watching, awed at its devastating power, listening to its terrifying sound.

A little while before the flood, eight refugees had crossed the Nam Wa to collect bamboo shoots, and the rains had deterred them from making the return journey in their canoe. But as the water began to subside, Kaw

Her, Kham La Vang and Lue Vang decided to attempt the crossing. Leaving the bamboo shoots with the other five, the three young men got into the boat.

At first it appeared they would, despite obvious difficulties, reach the other side. But they had underestimated the strong current, and all the material it was carrying in its swift flow. Suddenly something hit the side of the dug-out, overturning it and throwing the three men overboard. Their attempts to swim were in vain against such odds, and they were swept rapidly downstream; all three drowned. Only one body was ever found, nine days later and completely unidentifiable.

Kham La Vang was a refugee teacher at the camp school. He was married and had one baby son. The rumour of his drowning was in itself a bad enough shock, and later when his father came to school to confirm it was true, it was difficult to believe. Kham La had drowned, we would not see him again.

Long shadows

The cost of becoming a refugee is great. The cost of being one is perhaps even greater. Vang made the decision to leave Laos for an unknown, insecure and uncertain future. Yet that was preferable to remaining at home, with all its familiarity and all its fear.

There have been many changes since coming over the Thai-Laos border nearly six years ago. Children have been born here knowing no other home; some young and many elderly people have died. Others have married. For the women there has been the least obvious change of life-style. But for Vang, used to the hard physical work of

Nov 9th
Went up to Sob tuang with
Chris and Catherine, who were
holding clinics at the hospital
in the camp

Some of the patients

Lady of Hmong tribe

"Uncle"
probably smokes opium

rice-farming, growing crops and raising animals, the restrictions of a camp have robbed him of dignity and a feeling of a self-worth, drained from him the drive and motivation needed for work. Older men find such changes hard.

Uncertainty is the underlying fear and it filters into every corner of Vang's life. Why not smoke opium again? But opium is a false refuge binding him yet more and lessening his opportunities for being accepted by a 'third country'. Receiving countries do not want those who are opium addicts. Vang's attempt to alleviate the burden of his anxieties serves only to increase it. The rest of the family must wait until Vang has been through a detoxification programme. One son is already in the USA and writes frequently to encourage his younger brother to do everything to hasten the family reunion. The younger boy is pulled between loyalty to his parents and the desire to go and join his brother, to make a new start. He has studied hard at learning English, but with Vang's growing opium addiction has been told to leave school and stay at home.

Fear and uncertainty still cast their long shadows over this family. How will they make the seemingly impossible decisions facing them? What does the future hold?

Please do not forget

Dear Ruth,

I'm very sorry maybe I go to Chon Buri on 31 March. I had my name (on the list) last Friday. Oh, everything is confusing. I can't do anything. When you come please visit my father-in-law and his family. Perhaps I am far away. They cry very much. Oh dear, my family miss you very much, please do not forget my family. I leave my uncle in Sob Tuang. Maybe you will see my (empty) house, but can't see my family (any more).

Oh, goodbye,

Your friend,

Jei (Zeb Yang)

Inside story

'What is it like working with refugees?'

I have been here as an English teacher at Sob Tuang for twenty months now. During that relatively short period, I have experienced times of deep satisfaction, joy and challenge, but also of loneliness, sadness and difficulty. I expected no less—a blend of frustration and fulfilment.

'Working with refugees' means working with people... with families and individuals... with Yang Sao, Malee, Yia, Vang Pao—friends whose lives I have had the privilege of being involved with. For them, yes, God's love

has reached out. 'Working with refugees' means having an increased awareness of what these friends are going through, and feeling the agony of being unable to help at the point of their deepest hurt. Hours taught, medicines prescribed, kilogrammes of rice distributed—all are necessary, but the need for time, personal care, for a heart that listens and tries to understand, is a very real need too.

'Working with refugees' means feeling lonely. Yes, even with other English-speaking friends to live and work with. But if I didn't have the capacity to feel lonely or misunderstood or bewildered, how could I begin to understand or identify with the people at Sob Tuang?

'Working with refugees' means not pretending to be someone I'm not. How quickly 'love' and 'help' become over-used words. Human love soon cracks, and selfishness and unwillingness are exposed. It is easy to be 'tired' and 'busy' and to send people away: not from their homeland—that has already happened—but from care, real interest and true compassion. My desire to help must be daily grounded in God's love and strength which are so much greater than my own.

'Working with refugees' means feeling the tension of not really believing that the new life to which they go when they leave the camp is what is truly best for them. I hold the knowledge and feel the pain of seeing their life here and contrasting it with what they will encounter in fast-moving Western society. I can't explain the intensity of the adjustment which will be demanded of them. And even if I could, how could they understand?

'Working with refugees' means doubting that my drop of help is doing anything effective in such a vast ocean of need. Doubts are read by some as weakness. But I am glad I have doubted, because having done so, I believe more firmly that however limited the help I can give may be, it is real and valid. I came here convinced that God wanted me to show his love in action. I am here to teach, but first and foremost to care—to care through teaching for the sake of Christ.

Hua Hin
DECEMBER
Pale yellow, (and sometimes mauve) Flower .. possibly a creeper or runner, growing in abundance right down to the beach

Tear Fund is an international Christian agency engaged in relief and development projects throughout the Third World. The aim is to show God's love in action by providing both practical and spiritual help in areas of need worldwide. Tear Fund UK's involvement in work amongst refugees in Thailand began in November 1979: first in Sob Tuang Camp, Nan Province, in the north of the country, for refugees from Laos, and subsequently in Songkhla Camp in the south, for Vietnamese refugees. Tear Fund has worked through secondment to YMCA Bangkok and the Thailand Baptist Mission. Tear Fund workers have met needs for skilled staff in engineering, medical, educational and administrative positions.

Sob Tuang is one of seventeen camps in Thailand; Laotian refugees are from Yao, Lao and Htin ethnic groups, but the majority come from the Hmong hill-tribes. At the time this book was written (June 1981), there was great uncertainty about the future of Sob Tuang as proposals had been put forward to reduce the number of camps for refugees in Thailand from seventeen to three over a period of eighteen months.

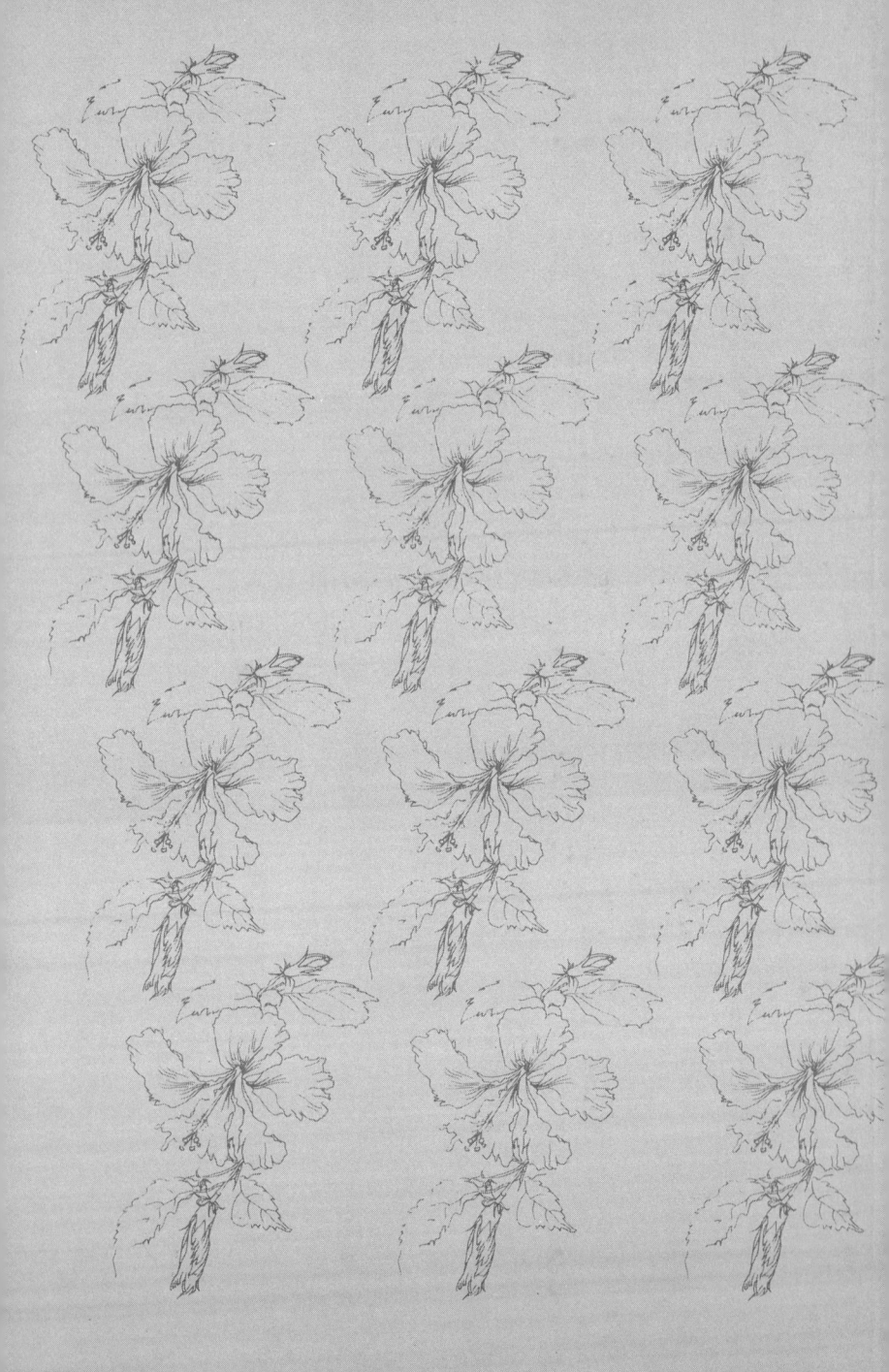